AR 48006 (30)

Dave's Down-to-Earth Rock Shop

by Stuart J. Murphy • illustrated by Cat Bowman Smith

HarperCollinsPublishers

LEVEL
3

To Down-to-Earth Dave and all the future
rock collectors he has inspired
—S.J.M.

To Eve and Peter
—C.B.S.

The publisher and author would like to thank teachers Patricia Chase,
Phyllis Goldman, and Patrick Hopfensperger for their help in
making the math in MathStart just right for kids.

HarperCollins®, ♣®, and MathStart® are registered trademarks of HarperCollins Publishers. For
more information about the MathStart series, write to
HarperCollins Children's Books, 10 East 53rd Street, New York, NY 10022.
Visit our web site at http//:www.harperchildrens.com.

Bugs incorporated in the MathStart series design were painted by Jon Buller.

Library of Congress Cataloging-in-Publication Data
Murphy, Stuart J., 1942–
   Dave's down-to-earth rock shop / by Stuart J. Murphy ; illustrated by Cat Bowman Smith.
     p.   cm. — (MathStart)
   "Level 3, Classifying."
   Summary: As they consider sorting their rock collection by color, size, type, and hardness, Josh
and Amy learn that the same objects can be organized in many different ways.
   ISBN 0-06-028018-2. — ISBN 0-06-028019-0 (lib.bdg.) — ISBN 0-06-446729-5 (pbk.)
   1. Set theory—Juvenile literature.   [1. Set theory.]   I. Smith, Cat Bowman, ill.
II. Title.   III. Series.
QA248.M78   2000   98-32128
511.3'22—dc21   CIP
                                                 AC

1 2 3 4 5 6 7 8 9 10
❖
First Edition

Dave's Down-to-Earth Rock Shop

Dear Josh, What's up? Here are some cool buttons for your collection. Uncle Nick

Dear Josh, Thanks for your letter. I'm off to the Grand Canyon. Uncle Nick

A package for Josh arrived in the mail. It was from Uncle Nick.

"Uncle Nick is always sending me cool things," Josh told his best friend, Amy. He gently shook the box. Something rattled around inside.

"Maybe it's a marble or a button," Josh said.

Josh collected buttons with funny sayings on them, and marbles too. He collected comics and baseball cards. In fact, he had the biggest baseball card collection on the block.

Josh ripped open the package. "It's a rock!" he announced.
"Why would your uncle send you a rock?" Amy asked.

"I don't know," Josh answered. He looked into the box again. Maybe he'd missed something.

There was a note from Uncle Nick. It said, "This is a rock from my trip to Hawaii. You're such a great collector, I thought you might want to try collecting something new."

"Rocks are everywhere," said Josh. "Why would anyone want to collect them?"

"Maybe it's a special rock," said Amy. But the rock didn't look very special. It wasn't shiny or pretty. It was just a dull, gray rock.

"Let's take it over to Dave's Rock Shop," Amy suggested. "I bet Dave can tell us something about it."

Josh and Amy hopped on their bikes. When they got to the rock shop, they saw all kinds of rocks on display in the window. Some were small, some were medium-size, and some were really big.

"How do you like my display?" a voice asked.

Josh and Amy turned to see Dave.

"It's great," Josh answered.

"Why are all the rocks in different piles?" Amy asked.

"I collect rocks, and then I organize them in different ways," Dave answered. "These rocks are grouped by size."

Inside Dave's shop Josh and Amy looked around.

"Wow," said Josh. "You really like rocks, huh?"

"Rocks are remarkable," answered Dave. "They can tell us amazing things—like how the Earth was formed and what kinds of plants and animals lived here long ago."

"What about my rock?" Josh asked. He held it out for Dave to see.

"Remarkable!" Dave cried.

"Can you tell us what kind of rock it is?" Amy asked.

"Of course!" Dave answered. "This rock came out of a volcano. It's called basalt. This book can tell you all about it."

Basalt starts as hot, liquid rock (called magma) deep inside the Earth. When magma is forced up through a crack in the Earth's surface, it is called lava. Lava cools and hardens quickly, forming different kinds of rock like basalt.

After their trip to Dave's shop, Josh and Amy started picking up rocks wherever they went. When they had a small pile, they decided to go back and see Dave.

They stopped at the window again. It was totally different. Now all the rocks were grouped by color.

"How do you like my new display?" Dave asked.

"Really cool," Josh answered.

"I never knew rocks were so colorful," Amy said.

"Rocks are made up of minerals," Dave explained. "The minerals are what make the rocks different colors. There are so many colors, it's hard work deciding what group each rock belongs in."

15

Inside the shop there were even more rocks than before.

"We've been collecting more rocks too," Josh said. Dave carefully examined each one.

"Remarkable!" Dave said, pointing to some strange outlines on the rocks. "These are called fossils. Your book will tell you all about them. Fossils are clues to the Earth's past."

Fossils

Fossil of shell

Fossil of leaf

Some rocks have fossils—traces of living things from long ago. After a plant or animal died, it might be covered by mud or earth that changed into rock over millions of years. The plant or animal would rot away, but its shape would be preserved in the rock forever.

"Clues? Does that mean we're kind of like rock detectives?" asked Amy.

"Yes," Dave said. "In a way, it does."

Soon Josh forgot all about his other collections. He and Amy spent all their extra time looking for rocks.

Rock heads!

They looked for rocks in the park, and in the creek behind Josh's house.

Josh picked up some ocean rocks when he went to the beach with his family.

Amy picked up some mountain rocks when she went camping with her aunt.

And Uncle Nick sent another rock, from his trip to the Grand Canyon.

Every Saturday Josh and Amy rode their bikes to Dave's shop. They helped Dave sort through his piles of rocks, and he told them things about the rocks they had found.

One Saturday the shop window was different again. Josh and Amy saw that the rocks were divided into three groups. Each group had a sign over it.

"How do you like my new display?" Dave asked.

SEDIMENTARY
Rocks made underwater from pieces of smaller rocks, plants, and animals.

METAMORPHIC
Rocks that have been changed from one kind of rock into another by heat and pressure deep inside the Earth over millions of years.

IGNEOUS
Rocks made when hot, liquid rock (magma) from deep inside the Earth cools.

"It's very scientific," Amy answered. "We'll have to look in the rock book to see what all those names mean."

21

As they helped Dave, Josh started thinking about their collection. "We have so many rocks now, I think we should put them in groups like Dave does," he said.

"We could group our rocks by size," Amy said. "Or maybe by color or type."

"There are lots of different ways to group rocks," said Dave. "One way is to group them by how hard they are."

"Aren't all rocks hard?" Josh asked.

"Some rocks are harder than others!" Dave said. "Your book will explain it to you."

MOHS' SCALE OF HARDNESS

Rocks are made up of minerals and they can be classified by hardness. Any mineral can scratch another mineral of the same hardness or softer. The softest mineral is talc. Any other mineral can scratch it. The hardest is diamond. Only a diamond can scratch another diamond.

It took Josh and Amy a week, but finally they sorted their whole collection by how hard the rocks were. Then they found a big box and divided it into five different sections. They carefully put all their rocks into the sections and labeled each one.

5-6

7-8

9-10

1-2

3-4

MOHS' SCALE OF HARDNESS

When everything was ready, Josh and Amy carried the box
to Dave's shop. They couldn't wait to show Dave how they had
organized their rocks.

But Dave wasn't there.

Josh and Amy waited all afternoon, but Dave never showed up.
Finally they figured out a way to leave their collection inside for
Dave to see when he got back.

The next morning Josh and Amy rushed over to Dave's shop. They stopped in front of the window to see if Dave had made a new display after his day of rock hunting.

They couldn't believe what they saw.

All of Dave's rocks had been taken away. The only thing in the window was their very own collection.

Just then Dave popped out of the shop.

"Here are my new rock experts!" he cheered. "How do you like the new display?"

Josh and Amy looked at each other and laughed.

"Remarkable!" they shouted.

In *Dave's Down-to-Earth Rock Shop*, the math concept is classifying objects in different ways. Putting objects in groups according to attributes like size, color, and composition is a skill used throughout mathematics and science.

If you would like to have more fun with the math concepts presented in *Dave's Down-to-Earth Rock Shop*, here are a few suggestions.

- Read the story with your child and list the different ways that Dave's rocks were grouped.

- Reread the story and ask the child how Josh and Amy sorted their rock collection. Did they do it the same way Dave did, or differently? Ask the child if he or she can think of other ways that the rocks might have been grouped, by weight, for example.

- Place a handful of blocks of different sizes and colors on the table and talk about the different ways that the blocks could be grouped.

- On sheets of different colored paper, draw a variety of shapes in different sizes—triangles, rectangles, squares, pentagons, etc. Help the child cut out the shapes and ask him or her to place them into groups by size, color, shape, or other attributes.

- Start a rock collection of your own. When the child has collected a number of rocks, talk about the different ways they can be put into groups. Can you think of a way to organize the rocks that Josh, Amy, or Dave *didn't* think of?

Following are some activities that will help you extend the concepts presented in *Dave's Down-to-Earth Rock Shop* into a child's everyday life.

Games: With a deck of playing cards or a set of dominoes, explore all the different ways that the cards or dominoes can be grouped—by number, by suit, by color, or any other way you can think of!

Marbles: Give the child two large loops made of string or yarn and a set of marbles of different sizes and colors. Have him or her place the large marbles in one loop and the small ones in the other loop. Encourage the child to explain the reasons for placing the marbles in one loop or the other.

More Marbles: Using the same loops, have the child put all the large marbles in one loop and all the blue ones in another loop. Let the child try to figure out where to put the large blue marbles. (Solution: overlap the two loops) Encourage the child to try sorting the marbles using other attributes.

The following books include some of the same concepts that are presented in *Dave's Down-to-Earth Rock Shop:*

- LET'S GO ROCK COLLECTING by Roma Gans

- FROG AND TOAD ARE FRIENDS by Arnold Lobel

- A STRING OF BEADS by Margarette S. Reid

Coral Limestone

Amy

Sandstone

Gruffy

Pink Granite

Dave

Diamond

Banded Ironstone

Sulfur

Amber

Nickel-iron

Obsidian

Josh

Silver

Diamond

Bituminous Coal

Mudstone

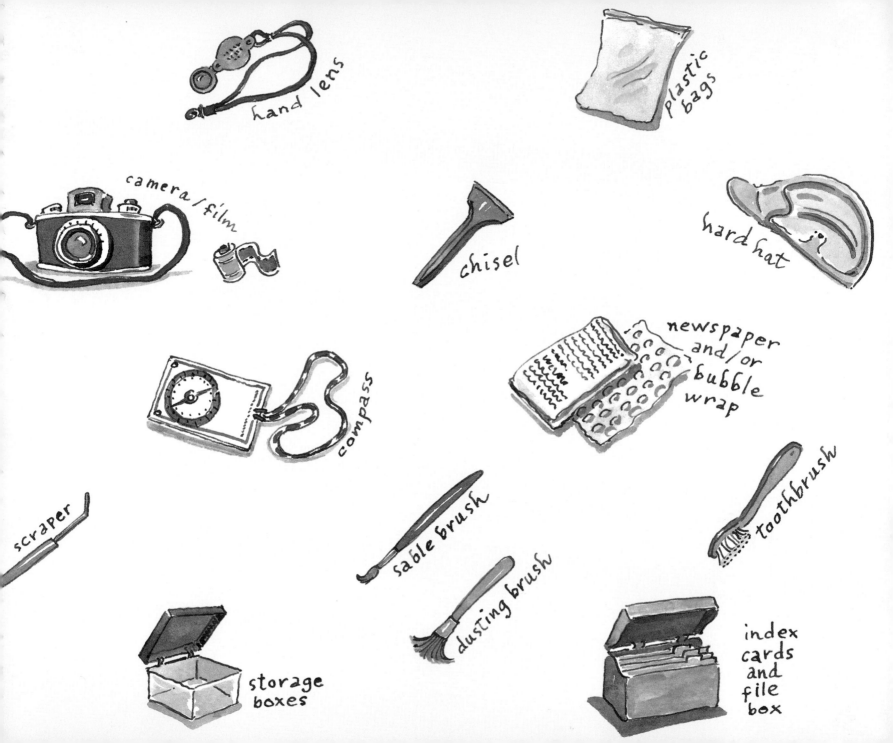

hand lens

plastic bags

camera/film

chisel

hard hat

compass

newspaper and/or bubble wrap

scraper

sable brush

dusting brush

toothbrush

storage boxes

index cards and file box